116 × 7/04
120 × 5/06 ✓8-06
136 × 8/08 ✓10-08
140 × 1/10 , 4/10
154 × 1-12,2-12
161 × 11/13 ✓12/13
161 × 4/13 5/14

74 × 9/08 -11/22
90 × 7/00
98 × 8/01

E
HEW   MH

King Midas and the Golden Touch

BY NATHANIEL HAWTHORNE

RETOLD AND ILLUSTRATED BY

KATHRYN HEWITT

HARCOURT BRACE JOVANOVICH, PUBLISHERS

SAN DIEGO   NEW YORK   LONDON

OTHER BOOKS BY KATHRYN HEWITT

Two by Two: The Untold Story

The Three Sillies

The Worry Week
Written by Anne Lindbergh
Illustrated by Kathryn Hewitt

Library of Congress Cataloging-in-Publication Data
Hewitt, Kathryn.
King Midas and the golden touch.

Summary: A king who wishes for the golden touch
is faced with its unfortunate consequences.
1. Midas—Juvenile literature. [1. Midas. 2. Mythology, Greek]
I. Hawthorne, Nathaniel, 1804-1864. King Midas and the golden touch. II. Title.
BL820.M55H49 1987   398.2′2   86-7681
ISBN 0-15-242800-3

First edition
A B C D E

The illustrations in this book were done in Winsor & Newton watercolor
and gouache on 90-lb. D'Arches hot-press paper.

The text type was set in Caslon 540 by Thompson Type, San Diego, California.

The display type was set in Erbar by Thompson Type, San Diego, California.

Printed and bound by Tien Wah Press, Singapore

Designed by Michael Farmer

Production supervision by Warren Wallerstein and Eileen McGlone

To my mother and father,
Mary and Hugh Moore,
with love

Hawthorne

With
very special
thanks to
Kathleen
Krull

ONCE UPON A TIME, there lived a king who loved
money. Gold was used as money in those days, and King Midas
simply adored gold. In fact, it was one reason he liked being
king—king's crowns are always made of gold.

When he was younger, Midas had enjoyed flowers and music.
But now when he looked at flowers, they only reminded him of
golden baubles. And when he listened to music, he heard only
the clink of one gold coin against another.

If Midas loved anything more than gold, it was his little
daughter, Marigold.

"Worth her weight in gold!" he liked to say as he tousled her
brown curls.

"Stop, Father! Don't muss my hair!" Marigold would cry.

Every day after a hearty breakfast, Midas and Marigold spent
an hour together in the royal rose garden. While the king
absently tended the roses and thought up ways to get more gold,

Marigold played with the royal pets—a golden retriever, a
goldfinch, a goldfish, and her favorite, the royal cat, Goldilocks.

Then, for the rest of the day, Midas would shut himself in his dark and dreary basement. There, under lock and key, he hoarded his wealth. He spent countless hours polishing and counting his treasures. He fingered gold coins in their bags, sifted gold dust through his fingers, and laughed at the funny image of his own face reflected in a huge gold cup.

"Oh, rich King Midas, what a happy man thou art," he would chortle to himself. The face in the cup grinned back. Midas wondered if the face was making fun of him. Or was it trying to tell him he was not as happy as he could be?

One day, Midas was whispering and laughing to himself as usual when a loud voice answered back!

"Are you *really* happy?" the voice asked.

Midas whirled around to see a radiant, glowing stranger. The king knew he had carefully turned the key in the lock and that no mortal man could have followed him into his storeroom. This stranger had to be a spirit with supernatural powers. Midas had read many stories of such beings, and he was unafraid.

"Are you happy?" the stranger asked again, gazing about the room. "Certainly you have riches, friend Midas. They must please you."

"Oh, this is nothing," Midas said, "compared to what I want. And it has taken my whole life just to get this much."

"Then you're *not* happy?" asked the stranger yet again. "What, pray tell, would make you happy?"

Midas paused and thought carefully. In all the stories, the magic spirit granted a person his or her every wish. Midas was not about to wish for something foolish, as all the people in those stories seemed to do.

"Tell me," urged the stranger.

"Since you ask," Midas began, "I'm tired of plotting new ways to get gold. Collecting my treasures takes up so much time. I wish—I wish that everything I touched would change to gold!"

"Ah, the Golden Touch," said the stranger. "No one's asked for that in ages. Are you quite sure this will make you happy?"

"I ask nothing else," said Midas humbly.

"Very well. Tomorrow at sunrise you will find yourself gifted with the Golden Touch. Good luck!"

The figure of the stranger became blindingly bright, and Midas closed his eyes. When he opened them again, he saw only one yellow sunbeam and, all around him, the glistening of his gold.

That night, Midas slept like a baby. Day had hardly peeped over the hills when he was wide-awake. He began to touch things—his alarm clock, his nightstand, his royal night-light.

To his vast disappointment, they remained exactly the same. How foolish to have fallen for a stranger's joke.

He pulled his blanket over his head and wept a few unkingly tears.
Just then, the day's first sunbeam entered the room, and the
blanket in the king's hands turned to soft gold cloth! The
Golden Touch had arrived!

Midas leaped out of bed. He seized a bedpost, and it turned into a lovely gold pillar. He pulled aside a curtain, and the tassel grew heavy in his hand—a mass of gold. He grabbed a book from his nightstand, and it became a splendid gilt-edged volume. The pages became thin golden plates, making the wisdom of the book disappear, but Midas was too busy putting on his clothes to notice.

He laughed with pleasure to see himself in a magnificent—though rather heavy—suit of gold cloth. He drew out the handkerchief dear little Marigold had embroidered for him. Now it was gold, with all the neat stitches in gold thread. He hoped she wouldn't mind.

When Midas put on his spectacles, the transparent glass turned into plates of yellow metal. For a moment he was sad—with all his wealth, he'd never again be able to have a pair of useful spectacles. But then he rejoiced. Think how valuable they were now!

Outside in the garden, where hundreds of lovely roses were in bloom, he went from bush to bush, touching everything until even the worms had turned to gold.

He had worked up quite an appetite by the time he was
summoned to breakfast. He hurried to the dining room,
accidentally kicking the royal cat on his way.

He sat down and awaited Marigold's arrival. He couldn't wait to tell her his marvelous news. But to his great dismay, Marigold entered the room sobbing loudly.

"How now!" exclaimed Midas. "What could make you so sad on such a beautiful—such a *golden*—morning?"

Weeping too hard to talk, Marigold showed him the solid gold cat she held in her arms.

"It's exquisite," the king assured her.

"It's *Goldilocks!*" the little girl screamed. "He's been changed into gold—my darling kitty!"

"Oh, dear," said Midas, who didn't know how to tell her that he himself had changed the cat. "Eat your breakfast," he told her kindly, "and then I have a surprise for you."

"Better than Goldilocks?" Marigold sniffled.

"Much better," said Midas, pouring himself a cup of coffee and marveling when the china coffeepot changed to gold. He lifted a spoonful of coffee to his lips. The instant his mouth touched the liquid, it became molten gold.

"Bah!" he snorted, spitting it out.

"What's the matter, Father?" asked Marigold, busy with her breakfast.

"Nothing, child, nothing," mumbled Midas.

He looked at one of the nice little trouts on his plate, then touched it. Its little bones immediately became golden wires, its fins and tail thin plates of gold—a very pretty piece of work . . . only King Midas, just at that moment, was extremely hungry.

He helped himself to a pancake, then a boiled egg. Both were heavy gold before he could take a bite. He stared enviously at little Marigold, who was eating her breakfast with gusto.

Midas snatched a hot potato, crammed it into his mouth, and tried to swallow it in a hurry. But he found his mouth full of hot metal instead, burning his tongue so badly he roared aloud.

"Father, what *is* the matter?" asked Marigold again.

"Oh, what will become of me?" groaned Midas, dancing around the room in pain.

Marigold ran to her father in concern. Without thinking, Midas bent and kissed the top of her curly head.

"My precious Marigold," he murmured. "Worth her weight in gold."

But Marigold did not make her usual answer. Alas, her sweet rosy face became a glittering yellow. Her beautiful brown curls took the same tint. Her body grew hard within her father's encircling arms. Little Marigold was a human child no longer!

"Oh, woe!" cried Midas.

He buried his face in his hands and wept uncontrollably. He wished he were the poorest man in the world if the loss of his wealth would make the faintest rosy glow return to Marigold's face.

"Are you happy now, friend Midas?" came a voice.

Through his tears, Midas once more saw the mysterious stranger. "No, I'm miserable," he wept. "Gold is not everything. I have lost all that I really cared for."

"You are wiser than yesterday," said the stranger. "Tell me, do you now wish yourself rid of the Golden Touch?"

A fly settled on the king's nose but fell immediately to the floor, for it, too, had become gold.

Midas shuddered. "Oh, yes!"

The stranger told him exactly what he must do. Midas bowed low, and when he lifted his head, the stranger had vanished.

The king grabbed a clay pitcher, which turned to gold, and ran down to the river, the leaves turning yellow behind him. He plunged headlong into the water without even taking off his slippers.

At once Midas felt a change within himself. With great joy, he
saw the pitcher turn back into clay. He filled it with water, then
climbed up onto the riverbank.

He noticed a violet and touched it hesitantly. It remained purple. He had lost the curse of the Golden Touch!

He rushed back to the palace. The first thing he did was splash river water over golden Marigold. Immediately the rosy color returned to her dear little face.

"Stop, Father!" she sputtered. "You're getting my new dress wet!"

She didn't know she had been a statue, and Midas didn't tell her. He just hugged her joyfully.

Next he sprinkled golden Goldilocks, who *hated* water and came back to life with a snarl.

Then Midas went outside and happily began spraying water on all the golden rosebushes. . . .

Many years later, when Midas was quite an old man and riding Marigold's children on his knee, he was fond of telling the story of the Golden Touch. It had happened to a man he knew, he said, and the children laughed to think that someone had been so foolish.

King Midas laughed too, tousled the children's hair, and told them how he himself hated the sight of all gold except their golden curls.